# THE ALMIGHTY BIBLE

### A BIBLICALLY ACCURATE GRAPHIC NOVEL

**The Israelites groaned in their slavery and cried out, and their cry for help went up to God. (2:23)**

 **Apple of the Eye**™

Apple of the Eye Publishing
© 2010 Apple of the Eye
All rights reserved.

Available on iTunes for your iPhone and iPad
or visit us online at:

# www.thealmightybible.com

malum
Animation works

Edited by Kevin O'Donnell
Illustration and Color by Malumworks
A Golden Dog Production
Book Design by Poets Road

# Foreword

Exodus is one of the most exciting and important books in the Old Testament, maybe even in the whole Bible. Its gripping story of Israel's rescue from slavery in Egypt is one of the first stories of how God saves people in the Bible (chapters 1–18). At a thundering and smoking Mount Sinai, God gives the Ten Commandments to Moses (chapters 19–24), and finally, God instructs Israel to build a Tabernacle (a dwelling place) to represent His presence among them (chapters 25–40).

Most Bible readers think of Exodus as the second book of the Bible after Genesis. It is actually, however, chapter two of the five-part book known as the Torah, or Pentateuch. The Torah was divided into five parts because no single scroll could hold the whole book.

Though Exodus is chapter two, it actually begins the main story of the Torah: the account of God's deliverance of His people from their bondage in Egypt. This is very important in how the people of God finally come into possession of the Promised Land of Israel.

The connection of Exodus with Genesis, which is the introduction to the Torah, is seen in the first few verses of Exodus (1:1–1:5), which lists the names of the sons of Jacob/Israel who moved down to Egypt with their families (see also Gen. 46:8). Genesis ended some centuries before the beginning of Exodus. At the end of Genesis, the people of God were an extended family; when Exodus opens, they had "multiplied so greatly that they became extremely powerful and filled the land" (Ex. 1:7). This language not only echoes the command to "fill the earth" given to Adam and Eve (Gen. 1:28) but also the promise given to Abraham that his descendants would become "a great nation" (Gen. 12:2). God had promised Abraham that He would "multiply [his] descendants beyond number, like the stars in the sky and the sand on the seashore" (Gen. 22:17).

Unfortunately, there was a problem. The Egyptians had enslaved all these people of God. When they first entered Egypt as an extended family, the Hebrews were honored because of the work of Joseph on behalf of the Pharaoh. But, as Exodus 1:8 informs the reader, a new king of Egypt came who did not know Joseph. Moreover, he was afraid of this large, foreign people within his own borders. Though not mentioned in the Bible, this fear may well have been kindled by the domination of Egypt at the hands of a foreign people known as the Hyksos in the 17th and early 16th centuries BC, some time before the events of Exodus. Whatever the motivation for the fear, the king not only enslaved the descendants of Abraham, Isaac, and Jacob, he determined to kill all the newborn baby boys, thus lessening the possibility of an armed resistance.

God, though, had other plans for His people. He enlisted people like the midwives to allow some Hebrew male babies to escape the slaughter. Moses was one of those babies, and the story of his birth is one of the most memorable accounts in all the Old Testament. After he was born and grew a bit, his mother knew that she could not keep his existence a secret much longer. What was she to do? She decided to put him in a basket made of papyrus reeds, caulked with tar and pitch, and then, she placed him on the Nile River to carry him away. To us, reading this story in the 21st century AD, her actions seem strange, arbitrary, and even careless. But we know from other comparable stories from the ancient Near East (birth legend of Sargon) that placing a child on a river was not turning the child over to chance but, rather, placing that child in the hand of God. And God, in this case, did a most miraculous thing: He brought baby Moses into the household of Pharaoh himself. How ironic! Moses, the future savior of Israel, was raised in the household of the very one who wanted him dead. And Moses's mother not only saw her son survive; she got hired to serve as his wet nurse.

At this point, the story moves quickly, and Moses grows into a young man. In a moment of rage at an injustice being carried out by an Egyptian on a Hebrew slave, Moses killed the attacker. This crime in the eyes of Egypt meant he must flee, so he found refuge in the land of Midian, a nomadic people situated on either side of the Gulf of Aqaba. While there, Moses gained a family (marrying Zipporah, the daughter of Jethro) and a relationship with

God. The historic moment comes as Moses was shepherding the flocks of his father-in-law near Mount Sinai (also known as Hebron). He saw a bush burning but not being consumed, and when he went to investigate, he heard the call of God. God then commissioned Moses to the dangerous task of returning to Egypt and demanding the release of the Israelite slaves from the allpowerful Pharaoh.

At first, he hesitated to accept this call. But after receiving Aaron's (his brother and future High Priest) help, Moses set out for Egypt to face a tremendous foe. That foe was Pharaoh—truly one of the most powerful people at the time. Even more frightening was the fact that Pharaoh was backed by dangerous forces: namely, the gods of Egypt. The book of Exodus treats these gods as real spiritual forces. After all, on the eve of the final defeat of these gods, God announced that He "will execute judgment against all the gods of Egypt" (Ex. 12:12). The reality of these gods also explains that once the battle began, the Egyptians had some power at their disposal. The Egyptian magicians, for instance, were able to turn their staffs into serpents in response to a similar act by Moses and Aaron (Ex. 7:1–7:13). After that, they could also turn water into blood (7:22). However, soon, their power ran out as plague after plague battered the people of Israel. After the final plague, the horrific death of the firstborn, the hardhearted Pharaoh finally relented, allowing the Israelites to depart. In celebration, Exodus 12 established an annual ritual, Passover, which has been celebrated throughout the millennia to this very day.

Even so, the drama was not over. After they departed, taking "gifts" from the Egyptians (Ex. 12:36), Pharaoh had a change of mind. He was embarrassed and angry and set out in pursuit. But God knew his plan. Although Pharaoh thought that he was setting a trap for Israel, God was setting a trap for him. Pharaoh would not receive glory this day; however, God would.

Thus, God ordered Moses to direct His people to a vulnerable position, a place from which they would have no escape because of the impassable sea behind them when Pharaoh attacked (14:1–14:4). We can imagine what went through Pharaoh's mind when he saw them there. They were easy pickings with no way out.

But when he attacked, God miraculously parted the sea, so His people could escape. Then, He closed the route through the sea in judgment on the pursuing Egyptians. As Moses would later sing, "The Lord is a warrior; Yahweh is his name! Pharaoh's chariots and army he has hurled into the sea" (Ex. 15:3–15:4).

It is this event that is the climax of God's saving activity in the Old Testament. Later, Israelites would look back and remember this event in a way that would give them confidence in the present and hope for the future when they faced seemingly overwhelming problems (Psalms 77). The prophets would later speak of a second Exodus when they waited for the restoration of God's people after He judged them with exile and captivity by the Babylonians (Isa. 40:305; Hos. 2:14–2:15). Finally, the New Testament authors saw the Exodus as an anticipation of the even greater deliverance provided by Jesus in His death and resurrection.

As momentous as it was, the Exodus event is just the beginning of the story of the book. The second major part of Exodus (chapters 19–24) tells the happenings at Mount Sinai. Moses took the Hebrews to Mount Sinai because that was where he met God in the burning bush. There, God made Israel His people, a nation chosen by Him to bring His blessing to the nations promised to Abraham in Genesis 12:3. On this occasion, He announced through Moses, "you will be my own special treasure from among all the peoples on earth; for all the earth belongs to me. And you will be my kingdom of priests, my holy nation" (Ex. 19:5–19:6). Further, He made a covenant with them; more specifically, He entered into a treaty with them. From now on, He would be their great king.

As king, He gave them His law. At the head of the law stood the Ten Commandments (Ex. 20:2–20:17). Although there had been law codes before in the ancient Near East (most famously that of the Babylonian Hammurabi), the Ten Commandments were unique. They were not case law but, rather, general ethical principles that would guide Israel in a proper relationship with their God and fellow human beings. But it is wrong to think that this law was the basis of the relationship that God had with His people.

No, that relationship was formed by an act of God's grace. For this reason, the law itself was prefaced by the statement, "I am the Lord your God, who rescued you from the land of Egypt, the place of your slavery" (20:2).

Following the Ten Commandments flowed the many more laws (Ex. 20:22–23:19). These were case laws. They applied the general principles of the Ten Commandments to specific situations. For instance, what did it mean to honor one's parents? According to Exodus 21:15 and 21:17, it meant that one should not hit them or speak disrespectfully about them.

Thus far, the book of Exodus has told us about God's great act of saving His enslaved people and also giving them His law. But Exodus has still more to offer as it describes how God will make His presence known among His people. In the last section of the book, we hear about the Tabernacle.

The Tabernacle was God's dwelling place on earth, a symbol of His presence among His people. The Tabernacle was a tent; thus, God would live like His people who were not yet settled in the land and had to move from place to place. The Tabernacle, though, was not an ordinary tent; it was the ornate tent of a king.

This final section of Exodus has three parts. The first part is the detailed instructions on how to build the Tabernacle (chapters 25–31). God insisted that Moses build the Tabernacle "according to the pattern I have shown you here on the mountain" (Ex. 25:40). God initiated the building of the Tabernacle; He gave the instructions for the design. He also provided the precious materials for its construction from the wealth given to the Israelites by the Egyptians as they departed (Ex. 12:36). He even gave the craftsmen their artistic ability (Ex. 31:6). Thus, the last part (chapters 35–40) details the actual construction of the Tabernacle, demonstrating that Israel built it to the exact specifications God had given them.

However, the Israelites did not just move from instruction to construction. The middle section (chapters 32–34) tells the regretful story of the Golden Calf. While God was directing Moses in proper worship, the Israelites engaged in false worship, thus bringing God's judgment on themselves. When Moses returned from the top of the mountain and saw this false worship, he broke the two tablets of the law and called those who were faithful to his side. The Levites responded to his call and went out and served as instruments of God's judgment, protecting the holiness of God. Little did the Levites realize that this act of faithfulness would gain them the priesthood. On this day, Moses ordained them in their office (Ex. 32:29).

Due to the Levites' actions and Moses's intercession with God (Ex. 32:30–33:11), God restored His broken relationship with Israel. He would continue to go with them as they traveled toward the Promised Land, and as we already observed, the book concludes with the construction of the Tabernacle (chapters 35–40). The book ends with a completed Tabernacle filled by the cloud of God's glory that represents His presence among His people (40:34–40:38).

Exodus is a magnificent book filled with suspense and excitement and narrating three of the most crucial moments in Israel's history. God created His people by delivering them from Egypt (the Exodus). He gave them guidance and structure by giving them His Law. And finally, He made His presence known among His people in the Tabernacle.

This book is not only stirring in the reading but in the seeing, as well. It lends itself beautifully to the visual presentation that follows. Let your mind be informed, your imagination be stimulated, and your emotions be stirred. Prepare to be captured by the words of Exodus as accompanied by the captivating images of the *Almighty Bible – Exodus.*

## *Tremper Longman III, PhD*
**Robert H. Gundry Professor of Biblical Studies**
**Westmont College**
**Author of *How to Read Exodus***

# Acknowledgments

Exodus, the second book of our series, has taken a great amount of work by so many people. Pastor Charles Kim has given wonderful insight, as has Professor Tremper Longman, III. Their knowledge and understanding of the Bible has been invaluable. Daniel Park and Dr. H. Joon Lee have also been deeply involved in the creation of this book. Their support, and the support of everyone at Apple of the Eye, remains a true blessing. Eunice Ahn has been a brilliant addition and has improved our editing and directorial process. Dan Cordie continues to make sure people everywhere hear about the Almighty Bible, and Martijn van Tilborgh works wonders on the Web and with our programmers. The artwork was created by Malum Animation Studios under the direction of Boo Kim. Mike Bundlie of Poets Road has been of immense help in the design phase of both the book and the mobile application. Dan Streckert has kept the text and images organized and triple-checked our text for any grammatical errors. Allen McVicker has spent endless hours introducing our books to the stores. Dong Chung and I have overseen all aspects of the production and done our best to turn out as good a book as we possibly can. Thanks to our great team, we believe we have succeeded.

Go to our website—www.thealmightybible.com—for additional resources or to iTunes to download our mobile application. We encourage everyone to sit back and enjoy the glory of Exodus. There is no need to rush. We have already edited the text, so that the core story is clear and intact. As always, we include the verses from which each page has been edited. We have edited our text from that of the *World English Bible* (www.ebible.org). Everyone on our team prays that every reader benefits from this book. Thank you for opening it up and letting God's words inspire you.

## *Kevin O'Donnell*
EDITOR

# EXODUS

# EXODUS

# MAIN CHARACTERS

### MOSES
The man appointed by God to lead the twelve tribes of Israel out of Egypt and into the promised land.

### MOSES'S MOTHER
When Moses was a baby, she took a papyrus basket and put Moses in it to save him from being killed by Pharoah's men.

### MIRIAM
Moses's sister, who followed Moses as he floated down the river bank; she told Pharoah's daughter that she would find a nurse for Moses.

### PHAROAH'S DAUGHTER
After finding Moses in the river bank, she had compassion for him and decided to adopt Moses.

### PHAROAH
The ruler of Egypt who was very stubborn and did not want to let the Israelites go.

# MAIN CHARACTERS

**JETHRO**
When Moses fled Egypt after killing an Egyptian, Jethro provided Moses with work as a shepherd. He became Moses's father-in-law.

**ZIPPORAH**
Moses's wife and daughter of Jethro. She bore him two sons.

**AARON**
Moses's brother who helped Moses lead the Israelites out of Egypt. He was appointed as the first high priest of Israel.

**JOSHUA**
The next leader of the Israelites who succeeds Moses

**BEZALEL and OHOLIAB**
The architects who were in charge of building the Tabernacle

All the souls who came out of Jacob's body were seventy souls, and the children of Israel were fruitful and increased abundantly and multiplied and grew mighty, and the land was filled with them. (1:5–1:7)

Now, there arose a new king over Egypt who didn't know of Joseph. He said to his people, "Behold, the children of Israel are more and mightier than we. Come, let us deal wisely with them, lest when war breaks out, they join our enemies and fight against us and escape out of the land." (1:8–1:10)

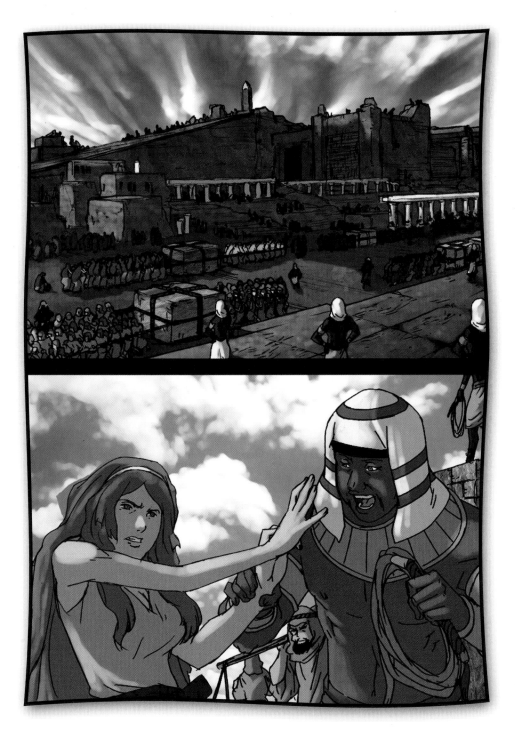

Therefore, they set taskmasters over them to afflict them with their burdens. But the more they afflicted them, the more they multiplied, and the more they spread out. The Egyptians ruthlessly made the children of Israel serve, and they made their lives bitter with hard service. (1:11–1:14)

The Pharaoh spoke to the Hebrew midwives, Shiphrah and Puah, and he said, "When you perform the duty of a midwife to the Hebrew women, if it is a son, you shall kill him, but if it is a daughter, she shall live." But the midwives feared God and saved the baby boys. (1:15–1:17)

The king of Egypt called for the midwives and said to them, "Why have you saved the boys alive?" The midwives said, "Because the Hebrew women aren't like the Egyptian women; they give birth before we come to them." Pharaoh commanded, "You shall cast every son who is born into the river." (1:18–1:22)

A daughter of Levi conceived and bore a son. When she saw that he was a fine child, she hid him three months. When she could no longer hide him, she took a papyrus basket for him and coated it with tar and with pitch. (2:1–2:3)

She put the child in it and laid it in the reeds by the river's bank. His sister stood far off to see what would be done to him. Pharaoh's daughter came down to bathe at the river. She saw the basket among the reeds and sent her handmaid to get it. She opened it, and the baby cried. (2:3–2:6)

Pharaoh's daughter said to her, "Go." The maiden went and called her mother. Pharaoh's daughter said to the real mother of the baby, "Take this child away and nurse him for me, and I will give you your wages." (2:7–2:9)

The woman took the child and nursed it. The child grew, and she brought him to Pharaoh's daughter, and he became her son. The Egyptian princess named him Moses, saying, "Because I drew him out of the water." (2:9–2:10)

When Moses had grown up, he went out to his brothers and looked at their burdens. He saw an Egyptian striking a Hebrew. He looked this way and that way, and when he saw that there was no one, he killed the Egyptian and hid him in the sand. (2:11–2:12)

Moses went out the second day and saw two Hebrews fighting with each other. He said to the one who started it, "Why do you strike your fellow?" He said, "Who made you a prince and a judge over us? Do you plan to kill me as you killed the Egyptian?" Moses was afraid, thinking, "Surely this thing is known." (2:13–2:14)

Now, when Pharaoh heard this thing, he sought to kill Moses. But Moses fled from the face of Pharaoh and lived in the land of Midian, and he sat down by a well. Now, the priest of Midian had seven daughters. They came and drew water and filled the troughs to water their father's flock. (2:15–2:16)

The shepherds came and drove them away, but Moses stood up and helped them and watered their flock. When they came to their father, they said, "An Egyptian delivered us out of the hand of the shepherds." He said to his daughters, "Where is he? Why is it that you have left the man? Call him, that he may eat bread." (2:17–2:20)

He gave Moses Zipporah, his daughter. She bore a son, and he named him Gershom, for he said, "I have lived as a foreigner in a foreign land." (2:21–2:22)

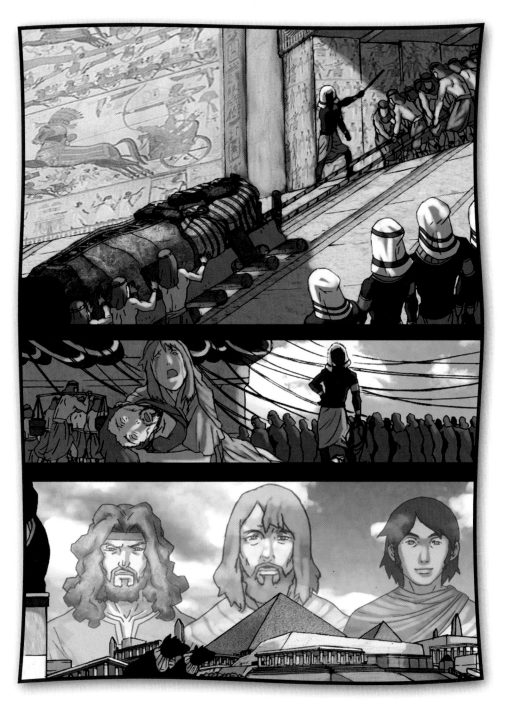

It happened that the king of Egypt died, and the children of Israel sighed because of the bondage, and they cried, and their cry came up to God. God heard their groaning and remembered his covenant with Abraham, with Isaac, and with Jacob. God saw the children of Israel, and God was concerned about them. (2:23–2:25)

Now, Moses was keeping the flock of Jethro (his father-in-law), and he led the flock to the back of the wilderness and came to God's mountain, to Horeb. (3:1)

The angel of Yahweh appeared to him in a flame of fire out of the midst of a bush. "Moses! Moses!" He said, "Don't come close. Take your sandals off of your feet, for the place you are standing on is holy ground. I am the God of your father, the God of Abraham, the God of Isaac, and the God of Jacob." (3:2–3:6)

Moses hid his face, for he was afraid to look at God. Yahweh said, "I have surely seen the affliction of my people and I know their sorrows. I have come down to bring them up out of that land to a land flowing with milk and honey; therefore, I will send you to Pharaoh, that you may bring my people, the children of Israel, out of Egypt." (3:6–3:10)

Moses said, "Who am I, that I should bring the children of Israel out of Egypt?" God said, "I will be with you." Moses said, "When I tell them, 'The God of your fathers sent me,' and they ask me, 'What is his name,' what should I tell them?" God said, "I AM WHO I AM. You shall tell them, 'I AM has sent me to you.'" (3:11–3:14)

"Go and gather the elders of Israel together. To the king of Egypt, tell him, 'Now please let us go three days' journey into the wilderness, that we may sacrifice to our God.' The king of Egypt won't give you permission to go. I will reach out and strike Egypt with all my wonders, and after, he will let you go." (3:16–3:20)

Moses answered, "But, behold, they will not believe me nor listen to my voice, for they will say, 'Yahweh has not appeared to you.'" Yahweh said, "What is that in your hand?" He said, "A rod." He said, "Throw it on the ground." He threw it on the ground, and it became a snake, and Moses ran away from it. (4:1–4:3)

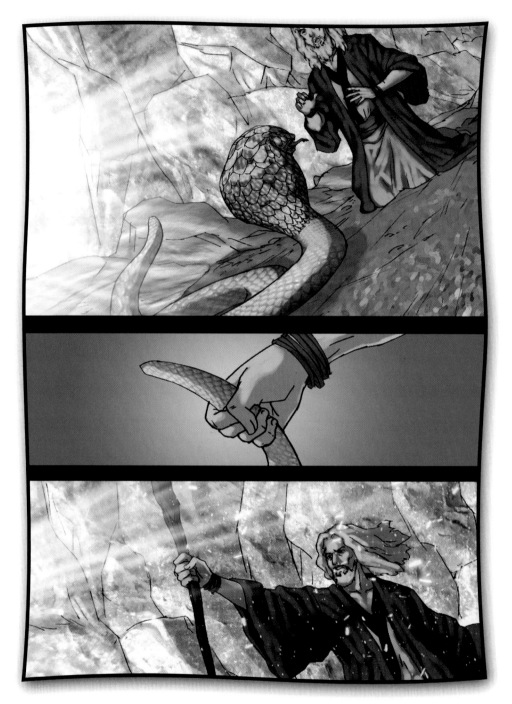

Yahweh said to Moses, "Stretch out your hand and take it by the tail." He stretched out his hand and took hold of it, and it became a rod in his hand. "That they may believe that Yahweh, the God of their fathers, the God of Abraham, the God of Isaac, and the God of Jacob, has appeared to you." (4:4–4:5)

Yahweh said, "Put your hand inside your cloak." Moses put his hand inside his cloak, and when he took it out, his hand was leprous, as white as snow. Yahweh said, "Put your hand inside your cloak again." Moses put his hand inside, and when he took it out, it had turned again as his other flesh. "It will happen; they will believe." (4:6–4:8)

Moses said to Yahweh, "O Lord, I am slow of speech and of a slow tongue." Yahweh said to him, "Who made man's mouth? Or who makes one mute or deaf or seeing or blind? Isn't it I? Go, and I will be with your mouth and teach you what you shall speak." (4:10–4:12)

Moses said, "Oh Lord, please send someone else." The anger of Yahweh was kindled against Moses, and he said, "What about Aaron, your brother, the Levite? I know that he can speak well. He will be your spokesman to the people. You shall take this rod in your hand with which you shall do the signs." (4:13–4:17)

Moses returned to Jethro and said to him, "Please let me go and return to my brothers who are in Egypt and see whether they are still alive." Jethro said to Moses, "Go in peace." He returned to the land of Egypt. Moses took God's rod in his hand. (4:18–4:20)

Yahweh said to Moses, "Go back to Egypt, do all the wonders which I have put in your hand, but I will harden Pharaoh's heart, and he will not let the people go. Tell him, 'Israel is my firstborn son and I have said, "Let my son go, that he may serve me"; and you have refused to let him go. Behold, I will kill your son, your firstborn.'" (4:21–4:23)

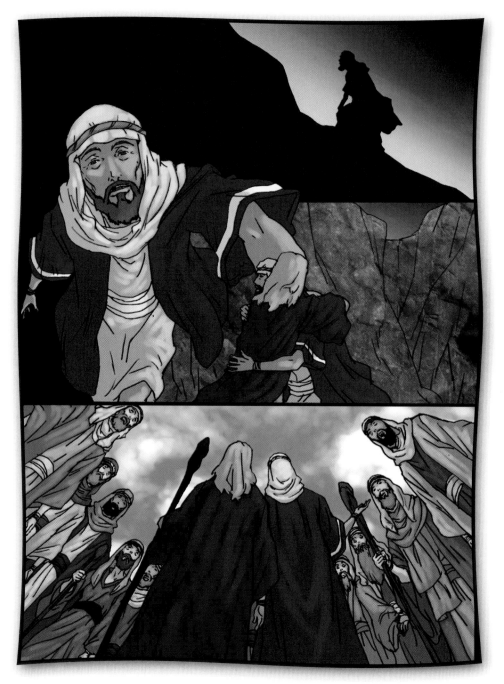

Yahweh said to Aaron, "Go to the wilderness to meet Moses." He went and met him on God's mountain and kissed him. Moses told Aaron all the words of Yahweh and all the signs. Moses and Aaron went and gathered together all the elders of the children of Israel. (4:27–4:29)

Aaron spoke all the words which Yahweh had spoken to Moses and did the signs in the sight of the people. The people believed, and when they heard that Yahweh had seen their affliction, they bowed their heads and worshiped. (4:30–4:31)

Moses and Aaron said to Pharaoh, "Yahweh, the God of Israel says, 'Let my people go, that they may hold a feast to me in the wilderness.'" Pharaoh said, "I don't know Yahweh, and I will not let Israel go." Moses and Aaron said, "Please let us go three days into the wilderness and sacrifice to Yahweh, lest he fall on us with the sword." (5:1–5:3)

The king of Egypt said to the Hebrews and those overseeing them, "Get back to your burdens!" Pharaoh commanded the officers, saying, "You shall no longer give the people straw to make brick. Let them go and gather straw for themselves." The children of Israel were beaten. (5:4–5:14)

They met Moses and Aaron, as they came out from Pharaoh, and they said to them, "You have put a sword in their hand to kill us." Moses returned to Yahweh and said, "Lord, since I came to Pharaoh to speak in your name, he has brought trouble on this people." Yahweh said to Moses, "Now, you shall see what I will do to Pharaoh." (5:20–6:1)

God spoke, "Tell the children of Israel, 'I will bring you out from under the burdens of the Egyptians, and I will take you to me for a people, and I will be to you a God; I will bring you into the land which I swore to give to Abraham, to Isaac, and to Jacob, and I will give it to you for a heritage. I am Yahweh.'" (6:2–6:8)

Moses spoke so to the children of Israel, but they didn't listen to Moses. Moses spoke before Yahweh, saying, "Behold, the children of Israel haven't listened to me. How then shall Pharaoh listen to me?" Yahweh spoke to Moses in the land of Egypt, saying, "Speak to Pharaoh, king of Egypt, all that I speak to you." (6:9–6:29)

Yahweh said to Moses, "Behold, I have made you as God to Pharaoh, and Aaron shall be your prophet. I will harden Pharaoh's heart and multiply my signs and my wonders. But Pharaoh will not listen." (7:1–7:4)

"I will lay my hand on Egypt and bring out my armies. The Egyptians shall know that I am Yahweh when I bring out the children of Israel from among them." (7:4–7:5)

Moses and Aaron went in to Pharaoh, and Aaron cast down his rod and it became a serpent. Then, Pharaoh also called for the wise men and the sorcerers. The magicians of Egypt did the same thing with their enchantments. For they each cast down their rods, and they became serpents. (7:10–7:12)

Then, Aaron's rod swallowed up their rods. But Pharaoh's heart was hardened, and he didn't listen to them. Yahweh said to Moses, "Pharaoh's heart is stubborn. He refuses to let the people go. Go to Pharaoh in the morning, and you shall stand by the river's bank to meet him. (7:12–7:15)

Moses and Aaron did as Yahweh commanded, and Aaron lifted up the rod and struck the river in the sight of Pharaoh and his servants, and all the waters that were in the river were turned to blood. (7:17–7:20)

The fish died, and the Egyptians couldn't drink from the river, and the blood was throughout Egypt. The magicians of Egypt did the same thing with their enchantments, and Pharaoh's heart was hardened. Pharaoh turned and went into his house. All the Egyptians dug around the river for water to drink. (7:21–7:25)

Seven days passed. Yahweh spoke to Moses, "Go in to Pharaoh and tell him, 'Let my people go. If you refuse, I will plague all your borders with frogs.'" Aaron stretched out his hand over the waters of Egypt, and the frogs covered Egypt. But the magicians did the same thing and brought up frogs on the land of Egypt. (8:1–8:7)

Then, Pharaoh called for Moses and Aaron and said, "I will let the people go, that they may sacrifice to Yahweh." Moses responded, "I give you the honor of setting the time that I should pray that the frogs be destroyed." Pharaoh said, "Tomorrow." (8:8–8:10)

Moses and Aaron went out. Yahweh did according to the word of Moses, and the frogs died. They gathered them together in heaps, and the land stank. But when Pharaoh saw that there was a respite, he hardened his heart and didn't listen to them, as Yahweh had spoken. (8:12–8:15)

Yahweh said, "Tell Aaron, 'Stretch out your rod and strike the dust.'" Aaron struck the dust of the earth, and there were lice on people and on animals. The magicians tried to produce lice, but they couldn't. They said to Pharaoh, "This is the finger of God," but he didn't listen to them, just as Yahweh had spoken. (8:16–8:19)

Yahweh said, "Stand before Pharaoh; say 'I will send swarms of flies on you; I will set apart in that day the land of Goshen, in which my people dwell, that no swarms of flies shall be there, so you may know that I am Yahweh.'" There came grievous swarms of flies into the house of Pharaoh and in all the land of Egypt. (8:20–8:24)

Pharaoh called for Moses and Aaron and said, "Go, sacrifice to your God!" Moses said, "We will go three days' journey into the wilderness." Pharaoh said, "I will let you go, only you shall not go very far away." Moses said, "I will pray to Yahweh that the swarms of flies may depart tomorrow, only don't deal deceitfully anymore." (8:25–8:29)

Moses went out from Pharaoh and prayed to Yahweh. Yahweh did according to the word of Moses, and he removed the swarms of flies from Pharaoh, from his servants, and from his people. There remained not one. Pharaoh hardened his heart this time also, and he didn't let the people go. (8:30–8:32)

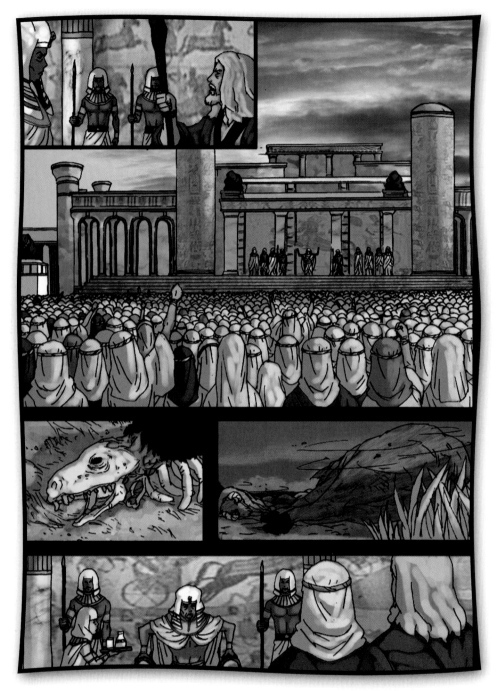

Then, Yahweh said to Moses, "Go tell him, 'Let my people go. If not, the hand of Yahweh is on your livestock, herds, and flocks with a horrible pestilence.'" All the livestock of Egypt died, but of the livestock of the children of Israel, not one died. But the heart of Pharaoh was stubborn, and he didn't let the people go. (9:1–9:7)

Yahweh said, "Take handfuls of ashes from the furnace, and let Moses sprinkle it toward the sky. It shall become dust over all the land of Egypt and shall be a boil breaking out on man and on animal." The magicians couldn't stand before Moses because of the boils. Yahweh hardened the heart of Pharaoh, and he didn't listen to them. (9:8–9:12)

Yahweh said, "Tell Pharaoh; 'I have made you stand to show you my power; as you still exalt yourself against my people by not letting them go, I will cause a horrible hail, such as has not been in Egypt. Every man and animal that is found in the field, the hail shall come down on them, and they shall die.'" (9:13–9:19)

Those who feared Yahweh sent their servants and livestock into the houses. Whoever didn't respect Yahweh left his in the field. Moses stretched out his rod, and Yahweh sent thunder, hail, and lightning as had never been in all the land of Egypt. Only in the land of Goshen, where the children of Israel were, was there no hail. (9:20–9:26)

Yahweh said, "Go in to Pharaoh, for I have hardened his heart and the heart of his servants, that I may show my signs in their midst and that you may tell your son, and your son's son, what things I have done to Egypt, that you may know that I am Yahweh." (10:1–10:2)

Moses and Aaron went to Pharaoh, "Let my people go or else tomorrow Yahweh will bring locusts into your country, and they shall cover the surface of the earth and the houses." They left and Pharaoh's servants said to him, "Let the men go serve Yahweh, their God. Don't you yet know that Egypt is destroyed?" (10:3–10:7)

Moses and Aaron were brought to Pharaoh, and he said to them, "Go, serve your God." Moses said, "We will go with our young and with our old, with our sons and with our daughters." Pharaoh said, "I will not let you go with your little ones! Go now (only) you who are men and serve Yahweh!" They were driven from Pharaoh's presence. (10:8–10:11)

Moses stretched out his rod over the land of Egypt, and when it was morning, the east wind brought the locusts. They covered the surface of the whole earth, so that the land was darkened. Then, Pharaoh called for Moses and Aaron, and he said, "I have sinned; please forgive my sin and pray to Yahweh your God." (10:13–10:17)

Yahweh took up the locusts and drove them into the Red Sea. But Yahweh hardened Pharaoh's heart, and he didn't let the children of Israel go. Yahweh said to Moses, "Stretch out your hand toward the sky." There was a thick darkness in all the land of Egypt for three days, but all the children of Israel had light in their dwellings. (10:18–10:23)

Pharaoh called to Moses, "Go, serve Yahweh. Let your little ones go with you. Only your flocks and herds shall stay." Moses said, "Our livestock also shall go with us." But Yahweh hardened Pharaoh's heart, and Pharaoh said, "Get away from me! Be careful to see my face no more; for in the day you see my face, you shall die!" (10:24–10:28)

Yahweh said, "One plague more will I bring on Egypt; afterwards, he will thrust you out altogether. Speak now in the ears of the people and let them ask of every neighbor jewels, silver, and gold." Yahweh gave the people favor in the sight of the Egyptians. (11:1–11:3)

Moses said, "All the firstborn shall die of Pharaoh and of the livestock. But against the children of Israel, a dog won't even bark. Your servants shall bow down to me, saying, 'Get out with all the people who follow you,' and after that, I will go out." He went out from Pharaoh in hot anger. (11:4–11:8)

Yahweh spoke, "Take every man a lamb, and you shall kill it at evening. Take some of the blood and put it on the two doorposts on the houses in which they shall eat it. For I will go through the land and strike all the firstborn. When I see the blood, I will pass over you." (11:10–12:13)

This day, throughout your generations, you shall keep it a feast. (12:14)

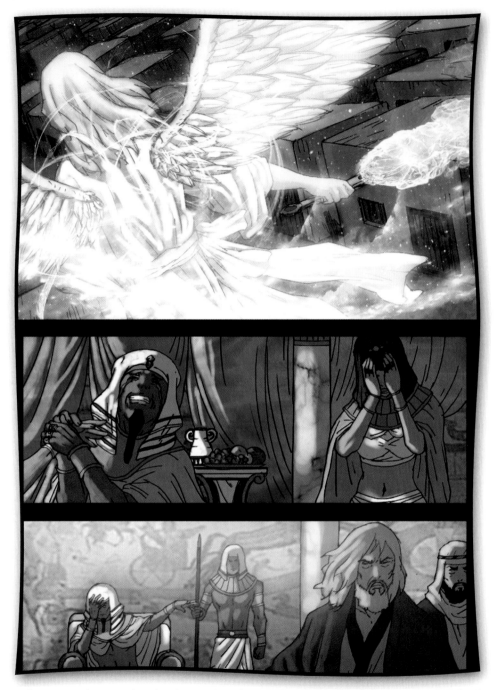

It happened at midnight that Yahweh struck all the firstborn in the land of Egypt. Pharaoh rose up in the night, and there was a great cry in Egypt, for there was not a house where there was not one dead. He called for Moses and Aaron and said, "Get out and go serve Yahweh! Take your flocks and your herds; be gone and bless me!" (12:29–12:32)

The Egyptians wanted the Hebrews to leave their land in haste. The children of Israel asked of the Egyptians more jewels, silver, gold and clothing. Yahweh gave them favor in the sight of the Egyptians, so that they let them have what they asked for. (12:33–12:36)

The children of Israel traveled from Rameses to Succoth, about six hundred thousand on foot, besides children. The children of Israel had lived in Egypt four hundred thirty years. Moses said to the people, "Remember this day. Seven days you shall eat unleavened bread, and in the seventh day, shall be a feast to Yahweh." (12:37–13:6)

God didn't lead them by way of the land of the Philistines, although that was near, for God said, "Lest perhaps the people change their minds when they see war, and they return to Egypt," but God led the people around by the way of the wilderness by the Red Sea. Moses took the bones of Joseph with him. (13:17–13:19)

Yahweh went before them by day in a pillar of cloud and by night in a pillar of fire to give them light. Yahweh spoke to Moses, "You shall encamp by the sea. Pharaoh will say, 'The wilderness has shut them in.' I will harden Pharaoh's heart, and the Egyptians shall know that I am Yahweh." (13:20–14:4)

Pharaoh said, "What is this we have done?" He prepared his chariot, and he took six hundred chosen chariots and captains. The children of Israel lifted up their eyes, and behold, the Egyptians were marching after them, and the children of Israel cried out to Yahweh. (14:5–14:10)

They said to Moses, "(Why) have you taken us away to die in the wilderness? We spoke to you in Egypt, saying, 'Leave us alone. For it was better for us to serve the Egyptians than die in the wilderness.'" Moses said, "Don't be afraid. Stand still and see the salvation of Yahweh. Yahweh will fight for you." (14:11–14:14)

The angel of God, the pillar of cloud, moved from before them and stood behind them, and the Egyptians didn't come near them. Moses stretched out his hand over the sea, and Yahweh caused the sea to go back by a strong east wind all the night and made the sea dry land, and the waters were divided. (14:15–14:21)

The children of Israel went into the midst of the sea on the dry ground, and the waters were a wall to them on their right hand and on their left. (14:22)

The Egyptians pursued and went in after them into the midst of the sea: all of Pharaoh's horses, his chariots, and his horsemen. Yahweh looked out on the Egyptian army through the pillar of fire and of cloud and confused the Egyptian army; they yelled. "Let's flee from the face of Israel, for Yahweh fights for them!" (14:23–14:25)

Yahweh said to Moses, "Stretch out your hand over the sea." Moses stretched out his hand, and the waters returned and covered the chariots and the horsemen. And the people feared Yahweh, and they believed in Yahweh and in his servant Moses. (14:26–14:31)

Miriam the prophetess, the sister of Aaron and Moses, took a tambourine in her hand, and all the women went out after her with tambourines and with dances. Miriam answered them, "Sing to Yahweh, for he has triumphed gloriously. The horse and his rider he has thrown into the sea." (15:20– 15:21)

Moses led Israel onward from the Red Sea, and they went out into the wilderness of Shur and found no water. When they came to Marah, they couldn't drink from the waters of Marah, for they were bitter. The people murmured against Moses, saying, "What shall we drink?" Then Moses cried to Yahweh. (15:22–15:25)

Yahweh showed Moses a tree, and he threw it into the waters, and the waters were made sweet, and Yahweh said, "If you will listen to the voice of Yahweh your God and will pay attention to his commandments, I will put none of the diseases on you, which I have put on the Egyptians." (15:25–15:27)

They journeyed on to the wilderness of Sin the second month after departing Egypt. The children of Israel murmured against Moses and Aaron in the wilderness, "We wish that we had died by the hand of Yahweh in the land of Egypt when we ate our fill of bread, for you have brought us out into this wilderness to kill us all with hunger." (16:1–16:3)

Then Yahweh said to Moses, "Behold, I will rain bread from the sky for you, and the people shall go out and gather a day's portion every day that I may test them, whether they will walk in my law or not. It shall come to pass on the sixth day that they shall prepare that which they bring in, and it shall be twice as much as they gather daily." (16:4–16:5)

As Aaron spoke to the people, the glory of Yahweh appeared in the cloud. Yahweh spoke, "I have heard the murmurings of the children of Israel. Speak to them, saying, 'At evening, you shall eat meat, and in the morning, you shall be filled with bread, and you shall know that I am Yahweh your God.'" (16:9–16:12)

That evening quail came and covered the camp, and in the morning, behold, on the surface of the wilderness was a small round thing. When the children of Israel saw it, they said one to another, "What is it?" For they didn't know what it was. Moses said to them, "It is the bread which Yahweh has given you to eat." (16:13–16:15)

The children of Israel gathered, some more some less. When they measured it with an omer, he who gathered much had nothing over, and he who gathered little had no lack. Moses said to them, "Let no one save any for later," but some of them did, and it bred worms and became foul, and Moses was angry with them. (16:17–16:20)

On the sixth day, they gathered twice as much, and Moses said to them, "Tomorrow is a solemn rest, a holy Sabbath. Bake that which you want and all that remains lay up for yourselves to be kept until the morning." They laid it up until the morning, as Moses asked, and it didn't become foul, neither was there any worm in it. (16:21–16:24)

It happened on the seventh day that some of the people went out to gather, and they found none. Yahweh said to Moses, "How long do you refuse to keep my commandments and my laws? Let no one go out of his place on the seventh day." So, the people rested on the seventh day. (16:27–16:30)

Moses said to Aaron, "Take a pot and put manna in it and lay it up before Yahweh, to be kept for generations." The children of Israel would eat the manna for forty years, until they came to the borders of the land of Canaan. (16:33–16:35)

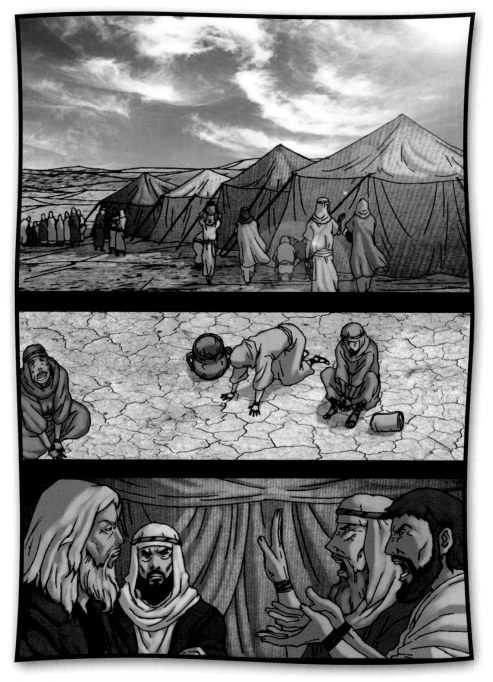

The children of Israel traveled from the wilderness of Sin and encamped in Rephidim, but there was no water. The people quarreled with Moses. Moses said to them, "Why do you quarrel with me? Why do you test Yahweh?" The people said, "Why have you brought us up out of Egypt to kill us and our livestock with thirst?" (17:1–17:3)

Moses cried to Yahweh, "What shall I do? They are ready to stone me."
Yahweh said, "Take the elders and take the rod. I will stand before you on
the rock in Horeb. Strike the rock, and water will come out of it." Moses did
so. He called the place Massah and Meribah because the children of Israel
quarreled and tested Yahweh. (17:4–17:7)

Then Amalek came and fought with Israel in Rephidim. Moses said to Joshua, "Choose men and go fight with Amalek. Tomorrow, I will stand on the top of the hill with God's rod in my hand." So Joshua fought with Amalek, and Moses, Aaron, and Hur went up to the top of the hill. When Moses held up his hand Israel prevailed. (17:8–17:11)

But Moses's hands were heavy, and they took a stone, and he sat on it.
Aaron and Hur held up his hands until sunset. Joshua defeated Amalek
and his people with the edge of the sword. Moses built an altar, and he
said, "Yahweh will have war with Amalek from generation to generation."
(17:12–17:16)

Jethro came to Moses at the Mountain of God. He said to Moses, "I have come to you with your wife and two sons." Moses went out to meet his father-in-law and bowed and kissed him. Moses told all that Yahweh had done to Pharaoh, all the hardships that had come on them on the way, and how Yahweh delivered them. (18:5–18:8)

Jethro said, "Blessed be Yahweh. Now I know that Yahweh is greater than all gods." Jethro took a burnt offering and sacrifices for God. Aaron came with all of the elders of Israel to eat bread with Moses's father-in-law before God. (18:10–18:12)

The next day Moses sat to judge the people from the morning to the evening. Moses's father-in-law said, "Why do all the people stand around you from morning to evening?" Moses said, "When they have a matter, they come to me, and I judge between a man and his neighbor and make them know the statutes of God and his laws." (18:14–18:16)

Moses's father-in-law said to him, "That is not good. You will wear away. Listen now. You shall teach the statutes and the laws, and you shall choose Godfearing men of truth to be rulers of thousands, rulers of hundreds, rulers of fifties, and rulers of tens." Moses let his father-in-law depart, and he went his way into his own land. (18:17–18:27)

In the third month after the children of Israel had gone out of the land of Egypt, they departed from Rephidim to the wilderness of Sinai, and there, Israel encamped before the mountain. Moses went up to God. (19:1–19:3)

Yahweh called to him, "Tell the children of Israel. 'You have seen what I did to the Egyptians and how I bore you on eagles' wings and brought you to myself. Now, if you will obey my voice and keep my covenant, you shall be my own possession from among all peoples; for all the earth is mine, and you shall be to me a kingdom of priests and a holy nation.'" (19:3–19:6)

Moses called for the elders and told them all which Yahweh said. The people answered, "All that Yahweh has spoken, we will do." Moses reported the words of the people to Yahweh. Yahweh said, "Tell the people to wash their garments; for on the third day, Yahweh will come down in the sight of all the people on Mount Sinai." (19:7–19:11)

"You shall set bounds all around, saying, 'Don't go up onto the mountain. Whoever touches the mountain, whether it is animal or man, he shall not live.' When the trumpet sounds long, they shall come up to the mountain." Moses went down from the mountain to the people and sanctified the people, and they washed their clothes. (19:12–19:14)

It happened on the third day, when it was morning, that there were thunders and lightnings and a thick cloud on the mountain and the sound of an exceedingly loud trumpet, and all the people who were in the camp trembled. Moses led the people out of the camp to meet God, and they stood at the lower part of the mountain. (19:16–19:17)

Mount Sinai smoked as Yahweh descended on it in fire, and the whole mountain quaked. The sound of the trumpet grew louder. Yahweh called Moses to the top of the mountain, and Moses went up. God spoke, "I am Yahweh your God who brought you out of the land of Egypt, out of the house of bondage." (19:18–20:2)

The people perceived the thunderings, the lightnings, the trumpet, and the mountain smoking. They trembled and said to Moses, "Speak with us yourself, but don't let God speak with us, lest we die." Moses said to the people, "Don't be afraid." The people stayed at a distance, and Moses drew near to the thick darkness where God was. (20:18–20:21)

Yahweh said, "Do as I say, and I will be an enemy to your enemies. Do not bow down to their gods. Little by little I will drive them out from before you. Moses came and told the people all the words of Yahweh, and the people answered, "All the words which Yahweh has spoken will we do." (23:23–24:3)

Moses built an altar with twelve pillars for the twelve tribes of Israel. Young men offered burnt offerings. He took the book of the covenant and read it. Moses took the blood and sprinkled it on the people and said, "This is the blood of the covenant, which Yahweh has made with you." (24:4–24:8)

Then, Moses, Aaron, Nadab, Abihu, and seventy of the elders of Israel went up. They saw the God of Israel. Under his feet was like a paved work of sapphire stone, like the skies for clearness. He didn't lay his hand on the nobles of the children of Israel. They saw God and ate and drank. (24:9–24:11)

Yahweh said to Moses, "Come up to me on the mountain and stay here, and I will give you the tablets of stone with the commands that I have written, that you may teach them." Moses rose up with Joshua, his servant, and Moses went up onto God's Mountain. He said to the elders, "Wait for us until we come again to you." (24:12–24:14)

The glory of Yahweh settled on Mount Sinai for six days. The seventh day, he called to Moses out of the midst of the cloud. The glory of Yahweh was like fire on the top of the mountain in the eyes of the children of Israel. Moses entered into the midst of the cloud, and Moses was on the mountain forty days and forty nights. (24:15–24:18)

Yahweh gave to Moses the two tablets of the testimony. When the people saw that Moses delayed, the people said to Aaron, "Come, make us gods, which shall go before us; for as for this Moses, we don't know what has become of him." Aaron said to them, "Take off the golden rings, which are in your ears and bring them to me." (31:18–32:2)

The people took off their golden rings and brought them to Aaron. He received what they handed him and fashioned it with an engraving tool and made it a molten calf, and they said, "These are your gods, Israel, which brought you up out of the land of Egypt." When Aaron saw this, he built an altar before it. (32:3–32:5)

They offered burnt offerings, and the people sat down to eat and to drink
and rose up to play. Yahweh spoke to Moses, "Go, for your people have
corrupted themselves! They have made themselves a molten calf and have
worshiped it and have sacrificed to it. Now, therefore, leave me alone that
I may consume them, and I will make of you a great nation." (32:6–32:10)

Moses begged Yahweh and said, "Repent of this evil against your people. Remember Abraham, Isaac, and Israel, your servants, to whom you said, 'I will multiply your seed as the stars of the sky, and all this land that I have spoken of I will give to your seed, and they shall inherit it forever.'" Yahweh repented of the evil which he said he would do to his people. (32:11–32:14)

Moses went down the mountain with the two tablets of the testimony. As soon as he came near the camp, he saw the calf and the dancing, and his anger grew hot. He threw the tablets and broke them. He took the calf and burnt it with fire, ground it to powder, and scattered it on the water and made the children of Israel drink of it. (32:15–32:20)

Moses said to Aaron, "What did these people do to you that you have brought a great sin on them?" Aaron said, "Don't let the anger of my lord grow hot." Then, Moses stood in the gate of the camp and said, "Whoever is on Yahweh's side, come to me!" All the sons of Levi gathered themselves together to him. (32:21–32:26)

He said to them, "Thus says Yahweh, 'Every man put his sword on his thigh, and every man kill his brother and his companion and his neighbor.'" The sons of Levi did so, and there fell that day about three thousand men. Moses said, "Consecrate yourselves today to Yahweh; that he may bestow on you a blessing this day." (32:27–32:29)

The next day, Moses said to the people, "You have sinned. Now I will go up to Yahweh. Perhaps I shall make atonement." Moses returned to Yahweh and said, "Oh, if you will, forgive their sin, and if not, please blot me out of your book which you have written." (32:30–32:32)

Yahweh said, "Whoever has sinned against me, him will I blot out of my book. Now go, lead the people to the place of which I have spoken to you. Behold, my angel shall go before you." Yahweh struck the people because they made the calf. When the people heard this evil news, they mourned, and no one put on his jewelry. (32:33–33:4)

Now, Moses used to take a tent and pitch it outside the camp. It happened that when Moses went out to the tent, everyone watched. When Moses entered the tent, a pillar of cloud descended. All the people rose up and worshipped, everyone at their tent door. Yahweh spoke to Moses face to face, as a man speaks to his friend. (33:7–33:11)

Yahweh said to Moses, "Chisel two stone tablets like the first, and I will write on the tablets the words that were on the first tablets, which you broke. Be ready by the morning, and come up in the morning to Mount Sinai, and present yourself there to me on the top of the mountain." (34:1–34:2)

He chiseled two tablets of stone like the first, and Moses rose up early in the morning and went up to Mount Sinai, as Yahweh had commanded him, and took in his hand two stone tablets. Yahweh descended in the cloud and stood with him there and proclaimed the name of Yahweh. (34:4–34:5)

Moses bowed his head and said, "If I have found favor in your sight, Lord, please go in the midst of us." Yahweh said, "Behold, I make a covenant: before all your people, I will do marvels such as have not been worked in all the earth nor in any nation, and all the people among which you live shall see the work of Yahweh." (34:8–34:10)

Yahweh said to Moses, "Write you these words; for in accordance with these words, I have made a covenant with you and with Israel." He was there with Yahweh forty days and forty nights; he neither ate bread nor drank water. He wrote on the tablets the words of the covenant: the Ten Commandments. (34:27–34:28)

When Moses came down from Mount Sinai he didn't know that the skin of his face shone because he'd been speaking with Yahweh. When Aaron and all the children of Israel saw Moses, behold, the skin of his face shone, and they were afraid. Moses called to them, and the congregation returned, and Moses spoke to them. (34:29–34:31)

## The Ten Commandments

**You shall have no other gods before me.**

**You shall not make for yourself an idol in the form of anything.**

**You shall not misuse the name of the Lord your God.**

**Remember the Sabbath day by keeping it holy.**

**Honor your father and your mother.**

**You shall not murder.**

**You shall not commit adultery.**

**You shall not steal.**

# You shall not give false testimony against your neighbor.

**You shall not covet.**

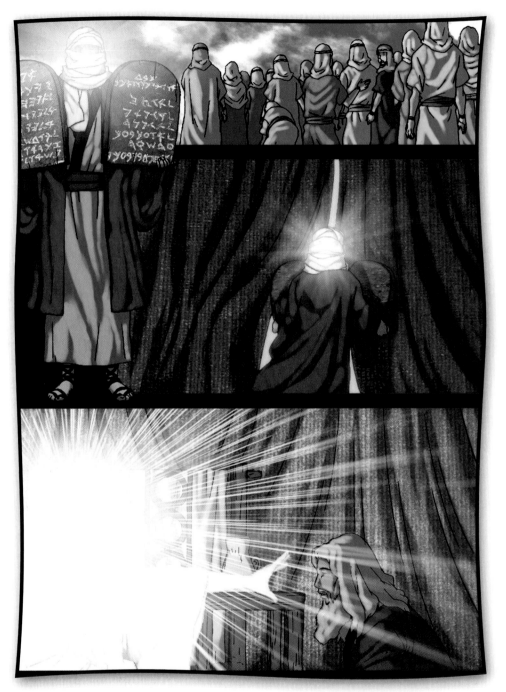

When Moses was speaking with the people, he put a veil on his face. But when Moses went in before Yahweh to speak with him, he took the veil off. (34:33–34:34)

Moses spoke to all the congregation of the children of Israel, saying, "This is the thing which Yahweh commanded, saying, 'Take from among you an offering to Yahweh: gold, silver, brass.' Let every wisehearted man among you come and make all that Yahweh has commanded." (35:4–35:10)

They came, everyone whose heart stirred him up, and brought Yahweh's offering. They came, both men and women, and brought brooches, earrings, signet rings, and armlets, all jewels of gold. The children of Israel brought a freewill offering to Yahweh. (35:21–35:29)

Moses said, "Behold, Yahweh has called Bezalel of the tribe of Judah. He has filled him with the Spirit of God, both he and Oholiab of the tribe of Dan, to make skillful works in gold, in silver, in brass, in cutting of stones for setting, and in carving of wood." (35:30–35:33)

Bezalel and Oholiab shall work with every wisehearted man in whom Yahweh has put wisdom and understanding to know how to do all the work for the service of the sanctuary, according to all that Yahweh has commanded." (36:1)

All the wisehearted men among those who did the work made a tabernacle with ten curtains; of fine twined linen—blue, purple, and scarlet—with cherubim, the work of the skillful workman, they made them. He made a covering for the tent of rams' skins dyed red and a covering of sea cow hides above. (36:8–36:19)

He overlaid the boards with gold and made their rings of gold for places for the bars and overlaid the bars with gold. He made the veil of blue, purple, scarlet, and fine twined linen. He made it the work of a skillful workman. (36:34–36:35)

He made a mercy seat of pure gold. He made two cherubim of gold at the two ends of the mercy seat. The cherubim spread out their wings on high, covering the mercy seat with their wings, with their faces toward one another. (37:6–37:9)

They made coats of fine linen for Aaron, and for his sons, and the turban of fine linen and linen breeches of fine twined linen and the sash of fine twined linen and blue and purple and scarlet, as Yahweh commanded Moses. (39:27–39:29)

They made the plate of the holy crown of pure gold and wrote on it "HOLY TO GOD." They tied to it a lace of blue to fasten it on the turban above, as Yahweh commanded Moses. (39:30–39:31)

It happened in the first month in the second year that the tabernacle was raised up. Moses spread the covering over the tent and put the roof of the tabernacle above on it, as Yahweh commanded Moses. (40:17–40:18)

He took and put the testimony into the ark, and he brought the ark into the tabernacle and set up the veil of the screen and screened the ark of the testimony, as Yahweh commanded Moses. (40:20–40:21)

Then, the cloud covered the Tent of Meeting, and the glory of Yahweh filled the tabernacle. Moses wasn't able to enter into the Tent of Meeting because the cloud stayed on it, and Yahweh's glory filled the tabernacle. (40:34–40:35)

When the cloud was taken up from over the tabernacle, the children of Israel went onward throughout all their journeys, but if the cloud wasn't taken up, then they didn't travel until the day that it was taken up. (40:36–40:37)

For the cloud of Yahweh was on the tabernacle by day, and there was fire in the cloud by night, in the sight of all the house of Israel, throughout all their journeys. (40:38)

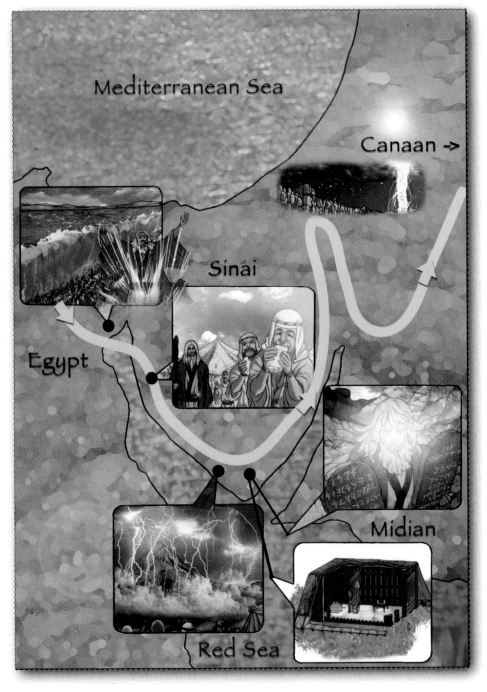

# The Tabernacle Tent

## The Tabernacle Tent

The priest would first enter the tabernacle into an area called the Holy Place, which had the **table of bread of presence**, the **incense altar**, and the **lampstand**.

Past the curtain was an area called the Most Holy Place, which had the **ark of the covenant**.

# The Tabernacle Court

### The Tabernacle Court

The tabernacle court consisted of a tent, a bronze laver, and a bronze altar. The court was enclosed by a fence, and there was only one gate.

The **tabernacle** was a tent structure and God's "place of dwelling," where He would come to meet His people.
The **bronze laver** was a place where priests cleansed themselves before entering the Holy Place.
The **bronze altar** was a place for burning animal sacrifices.

### Ark of the Covenant (37:1~9)
Residing in the Most Holy Place, the ark was made of acacia wood and overlaid with gold. Inside the ark were the following: a pot of manna, Aaron's budded staff, and the two stone tablets with the Ten Commandments.

### Table of Bread of Presence (37:10~16)
Made of acacia wood and overlaid with gold, this table had 12 loaves of bread that represented the 12 tribes of Israel. Only the priests were allowed to eat the bread every Sabbath.

### Golden Lampstand (37:17~24)
Hammered out of one piece of pure gold, this lampstand is also called the "menorah." Seven lamps held olive oil and wicks. The lampstand was the only source of light in the Holy Place.

### Altar of Incense (37:25~29)
This altar was made of acacia wood and overlaid with pure gold. The priests burned incense on the altar every morning and evening as a pleasing aroma to the Lord. The incense was made of four precious spices.

# Items of the Tabernacle II and Sacred Garments

**Bronze Altar** (38:1~7)
Located inside the courtyard, the altar was made of acacia wood and overlaid with bronze. On this altar, the priests slaughtered animals offered as a sacrifice and burnt them to cleanse the sins of the Israelites.

**Bronze Laver** (38:8)
In between the Holy Place and the bronze altar was a large basin filled with water. Priests used this water to wash their hands and feet as an act of cleansing themselves before entering the Holy Place.

**Court of the Tabernacle** (38:9~20)
The court was enclosed by a 7-foot fence made of linen hangings held by pillars. People could only enter through one gate, which was 30 feet wide. The gate was made with a curtain of finely woven blue, purple, and scarlet linen.

**Ephod & Breastplate** (39:2~21)
The high priest wore an apron-like garment called the ephod. On top of the ephod was a square breastplate with 12 precious stones that represented the 12 tribes of Israel.